BLESSED

A Laboratory Research Dog

BLESSED
A Laboratory Research Dog

©2021 Written by **Tamara Tokash** Art by **Romi Caron**

ISBN 978-1-60571-485-1

For more information visit www.tamaratokash.com

SHIRES ❦ PRESS

Manchester Center, VT 05255 | www.northshire.com

Printed in the United States of America

BLESSED

A Laboratory Research Dog

Written by
Tamara Tokash

Art by
Romi Caron

For John, My Shining Light

Lab Dog

The tip of my cold, wet, black nose begins to twitch and burn. It's from the chemicals in the room and the smell of the unwashed cage where I spend my days and nights locked inside. I have no blankets or toys. My smooth fur gets crumpled and worn from pressing my body up against the hard bars to keep away from the mess that's left behind.

I'm a laboratory research dog.

I don't have a name.

I'm trapped and scared.

My Beagle family and I were born for the purpose of being research animals. I was a puppy when I came to the laboratory. Beagles are selected as a lab dog because we are a friendly, easy-going, small breed.

People refer to me as PAA. These three letters are tattooed with indigo blue ink inside my velvety, floppy hound ear. In laboratories, scientists use animals to test how certain medications work before using them on people. Rabbits, guinea pigs, mice, monkeys and cats are also used to test for possible cures or to learn about any side effects from the medicines.

3

I am terribly sad and afraid – it's scary being a laboratory experiment; but I find comfort and some relief in believing – believing I will some day have a forever family.

My heart is filled with so much love to give and my soul is yearning to share it. I know that God hears me and it makes me feel better to know someone might be listening.

I don't have a family that loves me like a dog that's "free" or a soft bed to sleep on. I've never stepped foot outside of this sterile, brightly lit research room. My life exists within the four panels of the cold, hard wire cage. The air is thick and filled with chemicals. I have no choice but to eat, sleep and go to the bathroom here where I'm confined. This makes me feel so bad about myself. I try to pass the time by doing simple things – I sit, stand up, lie down, turn around and repeat over and over again. Sometimes I chew my feet because I'm sad and bored.

When I'm being used for a study, the research scientists take me out of the cage for a few minutes to either give me medicine or examine me to see how the medicine is working. Although it only takes a wee bit of time, it is the highlight of my day – to be out of the cage and get just a little attention.

While my days are excruciatingly long and nights are dreadfully lonely; I choose to begin every day and end every night with a prayer to my favorite saint, Saint Jude. He's the patron saint of hopeless cases and lost causes. My prayers are that someday I will have a family that loves me. I imagine walking with them through the forest, feeling the soft earth beneath my paws and breathing in crisp, clean air. Oh, and I dream of belly rubs, too. The only thing that helps me through the days and nights is believing that my prayers will be answered and I will find a forever family. I have faith.

Dreams

When the scientists leave for the day, it gets so quiet that it hurts my ears. I can hear my big heart beating inside my small body. It reminds me of all the love that I have to share and soothes me to sleep. That's when I begin to pray to St. Jude even more. I share my heart with him.

I close my eyes and dream of what it would be like if I wasn't a laboratory experiment trapped and locked in a cage. What would a day be like?

How would my heart feel? What would I do with the time I had left here on earth – how would I choose to spend it? How would I choose to act? I drift off and imagine being adopted by my forever family, running on the beach and leaving my paw prints in the sand. I leave behind the life of a laboratory dog, leave behind being just PAA.

The waves from the water are splashing on my fur and it feels so cool and refreshing. The warm gritty sand slips through my soft furry feet. As I skip past the sea grass it leaves a "whoosh" sound behind me. I am chasing after a seagull hoping he will want to play. He does! I run up to everyone I see and make friends with them all. I am so alive and free. AHHRRROOOO!

My forever family gives me belly rubs and throws squeaky balls for me to chase. I even jump in the salty water and put my face underneath to see what's down there. Wow wee: starfish, seashells and clams! I am having the time of my life – Yippie! My heart and soul are full of joy. I jump over a rock and land hard on the ground – suddenly I open my eyes and wake up just to realize it was all a distant dream.

I go to sleep the same way that I wake up – with faith and a prayer. My prayers are always the same: that I will be released from this life so that I can share my love with a special family. I refuse to stay sad about not having a forever family like "free" dogs do. Instead, I begin each day with a grateful heart and a positive attitude.

Day after day, year after year, I wake up hoping that today will be the day I could become a "free" dog. But everyday ends the same way. The scientists shut the lights off and close the big, heavy glass door of the sterile laboratory and leave us all behind in the dark.

My heart sinks when I think that I may never have a chance to share my endless love with someone special. Unlike the dogs in animal shelters, we are not allowed to be adopted. The researchers think we are wild dogs and would not be suitable family companions. My dream seems to be impossible, but I never stop praying, even as time slowly passes.

I have been in the laboratory for almost seven years and I am not young anymore. My body is fully grown, but the pads on my paws are still like a puppy's – tender and pink. That's because they have never touched the ground outside to become rough like a "free" dog's paws. I continue my daily prayer to St. Jude to rescue me.

What's in a Name?

Seven years is such a long time to be locked in a small cage. Thankfully, I have a good friend to keep me company. In the cage next to mine is my best friend, Hannah. She is also a Lab Beagle and was here long before I was. Hannah always asks me what the three funny letters in my ear mean and I never know what to tell her. No one ever told me the meaning of PAA so it is a mystery to me too. She has fun guessing to keep us entertained. "Maybe they mean Polite And Adorable," she might tell me. That one was funny. The letters in her ear were very faded so we don't know what hers could spell.

I like to lie on my back and stretch out to pass the time. I am always ready for a belly rub, even if there isn't anyone in the lab to give me one.

Hannah once said: "Maybe your letters mean Playful And Affectionate." She was pretty clever. Beagles always are. I told her that I was really starting to feel hopeless sitting here day after day. She told me to remain "Patient And Angelic" like my letters spelled. She had a million great ideas and it was so nice talking with her. I knew that one day I would figure out what my letters meant. For the time being, we both settled on something that everyone can agree with . . . Pets Are Awesome!

Changes

In the middle of one long September day, everything changed. I overheard the scientists talking about my group of dogs participating in what they called a pilot program that was led by a rescue group. A rescue group helps animals out of a bad situation and tries to help them find a better one.

They said, "Let's reconsider things and release this group of dogs to see how they do in the real world. Let's give them freedom and see what happens." Could it be true? Did I hear them right? I couldn't believe my floppy hound ears.

Yes, yes . . . it was true! The scientists said we were all going to be released from our lives in cages in the lab. We were free! I was free! Hannah was free!

Oh my goodness . . . we were all so excited. We were on our way to being adopted and becoming "free" dogs. Thank you for listening, St. Jude.

You must have heard me. AHHRRROOOO!

I will never forget the sound of the latch on the metal cage door unlocking for the very last time. A kindhearted Beagle rescue group worked with the laboratory. They gently and safely took us out of the research facility and placed us in a foster home, where we were put up for adoption.

Our hearts pounded with joy and our tails wagged in excitement.
Who would we meet? Where would we live? How would we spend our
days now? My mind raced with happy thoughts.

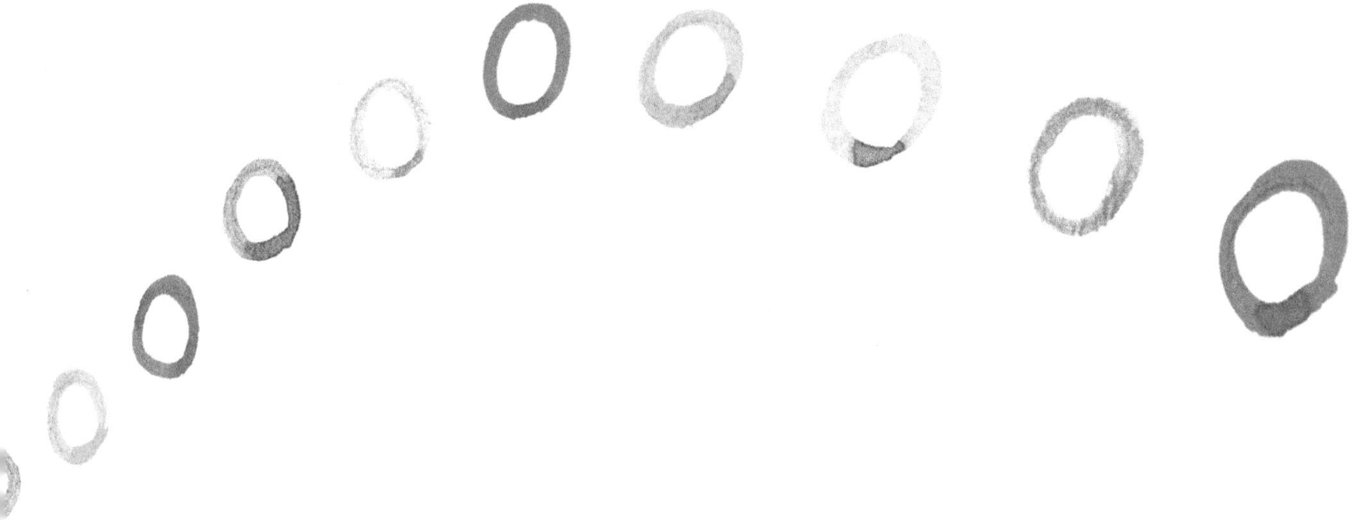

Doubts

In the foster home, a strange, new feeling came over me. For the first time ever, I started to doubt and worry about my uncertain future. My heart grew scared with the exact same questions that used to make me happy.

Who would I meet? Where would I live? How would I spend my days?

I was worried because life as a lab dog didn't teach us anything about living as "free" dogs. I was never in a house before. I wasn't house trained. I never experienced or learned how to walk up or down stairs. I didn't know what I could or couldn't chew on. I never met any children. I had no idea that the outside natural world even existed. The smell of fresh grass had never crossed my powerful, eager nose.

My mind and heart also began to wonder if I'd ever get adopted from the foster home. Who would ever want a dog like me? I had so much catching up to do. I wasn't a cute, little puppy anymore. Who would want a dog that needed to be taught so many things? Who in this universe would want a dog that was called a wild animal? Who?

I heard that a very nice woman was looking for a dog to bring into her family after her beloved dogs, Chloe and Max, passed. But she came to look at another Beagle at the foster home. He was not a Lab Beagle so I figured that he would certainly be adopted before me. Regardless, she was encouraged to visit with me since she was an experienced dog trainer.

I'll never forget that day. The moment we looked into each other's eyes, we knew we were meant to be together. I prayed so hard that she would adopt me. My heart was pounding so loudly from joy that I was sure she heard it, yet a strange sense of calmness surrounded me. She was so sweet to me. She had a loving smile and a gentle nature. Her family was there too and they were equally kindhearted.

I had found my forever home and I knew everything would be alright. This was really happening and my prayers were being answered. I was finally being adopted!

I knew that this had all been orchestrated . . . Thank you, St. Jude.

Freedom

The car ride to my forever home was like a dream. There were countless sights and sounds that I had never ever seen or heard. And, oh, the smells were amazing. I finally smelled sweet, fresh blades of grass. Beagles have exceptionally good sniffers, so everything around me filled my lungs with happiness. I felt like royalty. I was King Sam, the Regal Beagle.

AHHRRROOOO!

The first night with my forever family eased my doubts and healed my worried heart. Mommy gently placed me in her bed with lots of warm, cozy blankets. I never felt so loved and safe in my entire life. She whispered in my velvety ears, "We love you sweet Sammy. Everything will be alright." A magical feeling came over me. I felt my mind drift off into heavenly dreams and instead of my body being pressed up against a hard metal cage, it was now nuzzled up against my soft, warm loving Mommy's body. I could hear her big heart beating as I slowly fell asleep. I finally heard another thumping heart besides mine. Our hearts were one and I trusted her completely. At long last, my new life had begun.

The first few months were a difficult adjustment for me. There were so many times when I was frightened. I laid on a soft rug and whimpered a soulful cry. I had found my forever home but had no idea how to begin enjoying it. All those years imprisoned in a cage made it hard to deal with so many new things. I never felt these feelings before.

But Mommy knew exactly what to do and how to do it. I would often overhear her say to her son, John: "Everything works out when you do your best and have unwavering faith."

Every day Mom reminded me how special I was and that everything would be okay. She slowly introduced me to challenging new things that gave me lots of confidence. She also used canine enrichment games to make learning fun.

For many months, she carried me up and down the stairs, holding me close to her heart. I remember trying to climb the stairs by myself for the first time. I was terrified and fearful that I'd fall. Gradually I built stronger muscles and developed my coordination. I eventually made it to the very top!

Maybe the PAA letters in my ear meant Powerful And Adventurous. I was so happy that I ran down the steps and back up to the top again as fast as I could. I was Persistent And Alert. Is that what the letters in my ear meant? Maybe they meant Passionate And Agile? That's probably what Hannah would have said. She loved coming up with new ideas for my letters.

I was so happy to show my family my new talent. They were always so patient with me. Now they were so proud, too.

Thriving

My house training came with some accidents that embarrassed me. Fortunately, Mom never got mad at me. Her calmness, patience and love helped me stay focused and learn so many new tasks. I certainly enjoyed all of the yummy treats and praise she gave me as rewards for a job well done.

My family believed in me and saw things in me that no one at the laboratory ever did. People were always surprised to learn that I was once a laboratory dog because I adjusted so well from all the hardships I had overcome.

Mom said I was her miracle dog and began sharing my special story with everyone. I would listen carefully whenever she spoke. The gentleness in her voice touched my soul. I would hear her tell people how incredible it was that after being used as a science experiment for over seven years, I had so much love and happiness to give. She said I could have chosen to be resentful and aggressive, but I didn't. I believe that kindness is always the best choice.

With Mom's support, I learned how to walk on a leash, give my paw, sit, lie down and come when called. Most of all, what helped me to thrive was that Mom encouraged me to be me – a dog. She let me dig holes in the earth to bury my treasures, track scents of all sorts and chase after the critters that left them behind. She would take me on a bazillion "sniff walks" so I could read my version of nature's "pee-mails." I even learned how to count 1 . . . 2 . . . 3! Do you know that dogs can learn over 300 words and endless hand signals? You really can teach an old dog new tricks. Mommy said that I had a big heart and a healthy sense of curiosity.

I was learning to live the "free" life.

My family did everything together, and I mean everything. We would drive John to school and all of his activities. We would take long walks every single day, regardless of the weather. We had fun trotting through small puddles of water when we could find them. I remembered all the dreams I had when I lived in the lab. I wasn't splashing in the ocean now, but little puddles are so much better because I was with my forever family, and that's all that matters.

We shared our feelings and had long talks without using any words. We would even go on vacations together. Mommy always included me in her plans. It felt incredible to be needed and I knew that I was cherished by my family. I had a purpose.

My mind and body felt better than they had ever felt and I could out-walk any dog, even dogs half my age. Everyone would tell me that I looked like a puppy. My family noticed that when I slept, I wore a big smile on my face. It was because I was so happy and felt like I could leap over the big blue moon!

I was extra handsome when I wore my new, fancy collar that Mom had made just for me. It was full of exotic gem-stones. It was just magical.

I loved to eat and I sure did thrive. My favorites were wild salmon, organic apples, broccoli, blueberries and spinach. Mommy insisted that I eat only healthy food. She wanted me to eat real food, just like her, so I could live a long, happy life. She also fed me raw meat and raw bones, which is exactly what a wolf would eat.

Oh no! Why was she feeding me like a wild dog when I was a "free" dog? Was I getting sent back to the lab? Ah . . . silly me! I quickly learned that the healthiest way for a dog to live and thrive is to eat organic whole food, the way nature intended. My Mom even brushed my teeth after each meal. I was so grateful to know that she cared so much, which was another reason for me to smile!

Gosh, I'm blessed!

My Fur-Ever Family

When I was eight years old, my family adopted a Lab puppy. But she was not from a laboratory like me. That is just what they call her breed, a Labrador Retriever. John said that she was our other lucky charm. So he named her Clover. Clover looked up to me as her big brother and we always kept each other company. My Fur-Ever Family was complete.

Since I was originally a laboratory dog, I had missed out on learning how to play with toys, but I quickly learned how to play with other dogs. Mom called me her social butterfly. Clover and I both begged to go for car rides. They were always different, with so many interesting things to see and do. The smells of the world seemed to be more fragrant when carried through the wind and delivered straight to my well-developed sniffer. Barbecue season was a symphony of scents! Ahhh . . .

John was so kind to Clover and me. He never forgot to play and cuddle with us throughout his busy day. He made my heart feel all warm and fuzzy inside. We were the best of friends and life couldn't be any better. Mommy, Daddy and John always told me that I was a gift from heaven.

I never took this gift for granted.

Everyone had a lot of special nicknames for me. Mommy called me Sweet Sammy Sage because I was so loving and wise. She also called me Happy Boy because I was always so joyful. Daddy called me Smooshy-Smooshy because I was so cuddly. John called me Sam Mule because John has a great sense of humor.

My veterinarian called me Lucky Dog because most laboratory dogs don't end up with a life like mine. Others called me The Strongest Dog because I overcame such a hard past. My park friends would call me The Mayor because I spent so much time socializing. My other friends began to call me Old Man because I was 17 years old and aging fast. Seventeen years is getting pretty old in dog years.

THE MAYOR • HAPPY BOY
THE STRONGEST DOG •
HAPPY BOY • LUCKY DOG
OLD MAN • SAMMY MULE
SWEET SAMMY SAGE •

31

Circle of Love

I was having so much fun that I didn't realize how fast time was passing. Most of the sable brown fur on the top of my head had turned snow white. The brown and black fur on my back was now speckled with glistening grey. But there was still a small patch of silky brown fur at the crown of my head. It looked like a perfectly shaped heart! Mommy said that God placed it there.

My eyesight was beginning to fail, but I didn't let that stop me. Mommy, Daddy, John and Clover always guided me with gentleness when I needed extra help. What had not dwindled was my hearing, it was superb. I could hear Mommy cracking a raw egg into my food bowl from three rooms away. As I aged, I was encouraged to take more naps. The dreams I had now were far superior than the ones I had whilst in the laboratory. Although I was old, my spirit was young. I still felt like a pup, vital and energetic. I was determined to live my life to the fullest. I had a purpose; it was to share my unconditional love.

Every single day, Mommy and I would take our special walk in the park. It was our happy place. I had a jolly good time meeting up with my doggie friends, making new acquaintances and exploring fresh scents. Gradually our walks became shorter and slower but I looked forward to them just the same. As we trundled through the park we both felt joy and gratitude.

At home, Daddy gave me the best kisses, Mommy took care of me like a king and John gave me the world's greatest belly rubs that I had always dreamed of! John and I were kindred spirits. The PAA tattoo in my ear had faded and was now just a distant reminder of my past. Mommy told me that it was me, Sammy, that would be tattooed in her heart, John's heart and Daddy's heart forever.

Going Home

On October 28th, I peacefully crossed the Rainbow Bridge and went back to heaven. I passed at my home, cradled in Mommy's arms with John, Daddy and Clover right next to me. We could feel each other's hearts beat until my very last breath. It was like the first night I was adopted. Our hearts were one.

The circle of love that surrounded me that day was pure and infinite. Mommy's dogs, Chloe and Max, who died before she found me, were at the bridge to greet me, along with all of my family from the lab. I even saw my old best friend, Hannah. It was so great to see her again.

Mommy, Daddy and John still talk to me all the time. They know I'll always be with them. We will be forever connected by the light and energy of eternal love.

I learned so much on my 18-year journey. Find the good in every day and don't lose sight of your hopes and dreams. Let faith be your guide, even in your most challenging times. Find the light in the darkness. And never, EVER give up.

I think I finally know what the three mysterious letters tattooed in my ear mean.

PAA ~ Prayers Are Answered

My prayers were answered right up to the very end. You see, October 28th isn't just any day. It's St. Jude's birthday. I was home.

Prayer to St. Jude

Oh Holy St. Jude, Apostle and Martyr,
great in virtue and rich in miracles, near kinsman of Jesus Christ,
faithful intercessor of all those who invoke your patronage.
I have recourse from the depth of my heart
and humbly ask who God has given such great favor to come to my assistance.
I promise to make your name known and cause you to be invoked.

PRAYERS ARE ANSWERED

37

From Sammy

My family cherished me. I knew how much I was loved.
My heart was grateful. What an amazing, blessed life I had.
All those years in a cold wire cage led me to this happy ending.
I was born with a purpose; to give love to all of those around me.

My name, Sam means "God has heard."
St. Jude sure did hear me, too!
I thanked them every day for listening.

From the Author

From the moment I set eyes on Sammy, my prayer for him was that he would be afforded a full, healthy, happy and long life after spending so many years in the laboratory. My prayers were answered. In the end, that is exactly what he received.

We not only adopted a dog, but a dog's life that ultimately helped countless humans. We thanked Sammy daily for his service to the bio-medical community. After sacrificing seven years to science, he enjoyed eleven years of unconditional love.

He was a remarkable dog that taught many people the importance of gratitude, kindness and perseverance. My heart will always yearn for him, yet I know his beautiful spirit lives on and guides us all. I hope Sammy's story inspires you too!

How You Can Make a Difference

Adopt a Rescue Dog— adoptapet.com/dog-adoption

American Holistic Veterinary Medical Association— www.ahvma.org

American Society for the Prevention of Cruelty to Animals— www.aspca.org

Beagle Rescue and Freedom Project— bfp.org

Beagle Rescue League— beaglerescueleague.org/lab-to-leash

Best Friends— bestfriends.org

Happy Paws Rescue Inc.— happypawsrescue.org

Home For Good Dog Rescue— homeforgooddogs.org

Humane Society International— hsi.org/issues/animal-testing

Humane Society of the United States— humanesociety.org

Kindness Ranch— kindnessranch.org

Petfinder— petfinder.com

White Coat Waste Project— whitecoatwaste.org

Inquire with your local rescue groups, some work directly with research laboratories!

Other Resources

Animal Legal Defense Fund— aldf.org

Answers Pet Food— answerspetfood.com

Cruelty Free International— crueltyfreeinternational.org

Cruelty-Free Kitty— crueltyfreekitty.com

Diggin' Your Dog— digginyourdog.com/giving-back

Dog Cognition Lab— dogcognition.weebly.com

European Coalition to End Animal Experiments— eceae.org

Johns Hopkins Center for Alternatives to Animal Testing— caat.jhsph.edu/about

Leaping Bunny Program— leapingbunny.org

National Anti-Vivisection Society— navs.org

Puppy Leaks— puppyleaks.com/canine-enrichment

Physicians Committee for Responsible Medicine— pcrm.org/ethical-science

St. Jude Children's Research Hospital— stjude.org

Thrive Causemetics— thrivecausemetics.com/

About the Illustrator

Romi Caron is a professional, award-winning illustrator with more than 80 published books. She was born in the Czech Republic and studied art at the University of Fine Arts in Prague. Her drawing style and inspiration for nature scenes comes from daily walks in Gatineau Provincial Park, situated just a few steps from her home. She shares her knowledge of art in local schools by teaching special art classes. She lives with her family in the Ottawa region of Canada.

About the Author

Blessed is Tamara Tokash's first book. Tamara has over 30 years experience as a dog wellness expert. She possesses a keen understanding of canine behavior and the deep love and connection between dogs and humans. Her insights empower people to see the world through the lens of a dog, helping them both reach their full potential. Tamara's deep-rooted quest is to restore the integrity of a dog's life – mind, body and spirit – through education, lectures and private consulting. Tamara lives in New Jersey with her family.

In a perfect world, every dog would have a child like John in their life.
His loving nature and effortless compassion is what made Sammy flourish.
Of all John's impressive traits, the one I admire most is the love and respect
he unconditionally bestows upon animals.

Dogs are magical beings that are sent here for a paramount purpose.
Make time for your dog every day. Step away from the rush of the world
and be present with your beloved dog. Cherish the sacred contract you have with them,
they are one of our wisest teachers.

CPSIA information can be obtained
at www.ICGtesting.com
Printed in the USA
LVHW072317290321
682890LV00023B/1103